COFFEE
The Magic Drink

Milo Molina
Edith Molina
Kelowna, B.C. Canada
2013

ON THE COVER:

"Coffee overlooking Okanagan Lake"
This image was taken at the Kelowna City Park, overlooking Okanagan Lake, on a spring afternoon.
Kelowna, BC is a beautiful and vibrant city!

Library and Archives Canada Cataloguing in Publication
Coffee: The Magic Drink
Milo Molina and Edith Molina
ISBN 978-0-9738692-4-8
A catalog record for this publication is available from the National Library of Canada.

Acknowledgements

Very special thanks to:

Tisha Kalmanovitch for her help and guidance with the text.
Beverly Mallett, Alana Turigan and Norbert Spyth for
proofreading.
Adan Juarez for the drawings.
Haibo Du for the photo on page 66.

The Authors

Milo Molina was born in Mexico and graduated from National
Autonomous University of Mexico with a degree in Economics.
He is a traveller and has a great passion for coffee. He is also a
collector of coffee memorabilia and books about coffee. Wife
and co-author Edith Molina is a declared coffee lover who
learned to love and enjoy coffee a long time ago from her
father. The kitchen has been her home laboratory where she
learned and practised using different coffee makers, brewing
methods and used coffee as an ingredient for desserts and other
foods.

Another book by Milo Molina and Edith Molina

El Placer de un Café, 2006.

Kypogo the coffee drinker dragon is quite dominant and friendly. He and his wife Karmela show you how they prepare their morning coffee on page 69.

Contents

Introduction

One of the pleasures of waking up in the morning is to smell the aroma of fresh coffee. There is nothing like a cup of delicious coffee to start the day. Its aroma, heat and flavour comfort and encourage us to face the daily tasks with more enthusiasm.

Since its origin, the taste of this drink has fascinated the world. At first, coffee was an expensive luxury that only a few could enjoy; today, it is a very popular and affordable drink for everyone. As we know, the preparation of this magical drink is not complicated and only requires a combination of freshly roasted and ground coffee beans and water in suitable proportions. Drinking a cup of coffee in the morning or at any time is a pleasure, a habit and a ritual.

"*COFFEE The Magic Drink*" will not only serve as a practical guide to help you prepare the best cup of gourmet coffee, but it will introduce you to the world of espresso, a drink that serves as a basis for preparing cappuccino, mocha and latté. The book also describes the different kinds of coffee beans, the proper way to roast and grind them, the types of coffee makers, and other details that will enable you to prepare these superb drinks at home.

You will also find many recipes for fancy coffee drinks and for delicious desserts made with coffee: Café a la Diabla accompanied by Tiramisu, Viennese Coffee with coconut muffins, or a Mocha Soda, a cold drink that is very different from conventional ones, and absolutely delicious.

The book ends with some coffee legends and curiosities as well as links to websites that provide a vast array of information about coffee.

You are encouraged to travel via these pages through the world of coffee and to practise some of the most popular methods for its preparation, so that you may share pleasant experiences with family and friends over a good coffee.

"Oh! I enjoy my mornings with a simple cup of coffee"

Fascination with Coffee

People from around the world have been enthralled with this magic drink. Part of its allure is that it can be prepared and enjoyed in different forms and styles, as you will learn by reading this book.

Coffee, soccer, and samba are the three great passions of Brazilians. They take their *"cafezinho"* under any pretext and at any time of day. They prefer it pure and served in small cups. So important is coffee in the lives of Brazilians that the Post Office of Brazil launched a stamp impregnated with the aroma of coffee. The smell of Brazilian coffee may reach the entire world!

In Vienna, for example, coffee is a tradition as are coffee houses, where the Viennese discuss the events of the day, usually with one cup of coffee followed by another, and accompanied by delicious pastries.

For the French, the day starts with a cup of *"café au lait"* and a croissant. Later they might meet up at a local bistro or cafe where the main topics of conversation are politics, love and business. In France, as elsewhere, such cafe conversations have inspired the arts: painting, poetry and music.

In Italy, the tourist is fascinated when he enters some of the coffee bars that exist everywhere. The sound of the espresso coffee machines does not stop and to try a Roman espresso or a cappuccino is an experience of taste and delight.

The Portuguese, too, love their coffee. In Lisbon, the aroma of flavoured coffee permeates the old restaurants and Bohemian cafes from which you can also enjoy the haunting strains of

Fado music and the beautiful tile murals that adorn many cafe walls.

For many Argentinians, the morning starts with a *"cortado"* a black coffee with a little milk, exquisite *"medias lunas"*, croissants, and their favorite newspapers, *"El Clarín"* or *"La Nacion"*.

In Colombia, they call coffee *"tinto"*, which they like black with possibly some sugar and served in small cups called *"pocillos"*. Colombians drink coffee all day long.

In Mexico, many cafes are famous as centres of friendship and conversation. *"La Parroquia"* in Veracruz is one such Mexican cafe where people enjoy both coffee and the very special way the waiters serve it.

In the Middle East, the Arabs prepare a thick black beverage that is consumed throughout the day, wherever they might be. Merchants offer it to their customers and they feel offended if it is rejected.

Chinese people are starting to exchange their traditional tea for coffee. Part of this change is due to Starbucks, which has opened hundreds of outlets in major cities throughout China.

No other countries, however, can compare to the United States and Canada in coffee matters. In these countries, for more than two decades, the coffee mania has been unabated. North Americans have rediscovered coffee. Coffee bars, coffee houses and specialty shops have sprouted up like mushrooms everywhere. In these establishments, you can find a wide variety of coffee beans from all coffee-growing regions of the world. Coffee lovers are amazed to learn that there are more than 40 kinds of coffee to choose from!

There is a real craze for trying different types of coffee! People have expanded their coffee experience to include espresso, cappuccino, café latté, and mocha, drinks that can be served hot or cold. Moreover, in some places it is still fashionable to add flavoured syrup just before serving. The flavours that are in greatest demand are amaretto, hazelnut, vanilla and Irish cream.

Coffee drinkers everywhere have become more discerning about the quality of the raw materials they use, radically changing from instant coffee or canned and ground, to gourmet coffee, as its freshly roasted and ground beans produce a more fragrant and delicious beverage.

If your world has been shattered, have a coffee!
If your wife gone away, have a coffee!
If you lost your job, have a coffee!
If you are very happy, invite a friend for a cup of coffee!

About Coffee

People mention coffee every day. Here are some phrases which are commonly heard:

Let's grab a coffee!

Would you care for a cup of coffee?

Let's have a cup of coffee.

Don't worry. Do you want some coffee?

I was quietly sipping a cup of coffee when I thought of her again.

A good cup of coffee can mitigate any problem.

That place was very nice, wonderful, but I could not get a decent cup of coffee there.

I was so nervous I could not even hold a cup of coffee steady.

John starts the day with a cup of coffee and his favorite newspaper.

Let's meet for coffee.

Here, in this place, you breathe coffee!

What would life be without a cup of coffee?

The smell of coffee in the morning is like heaven and it helps me wake up.

Would you like a cup of coffee, dear?

Coffee Quotes

Here are some great quotes about coffee by famous and unknown people.

"Retirement is one giant coffee break." Unknown author.

"If I were your wife, I would put poison in your coffee." "And if I were your husband, I would drink it." Nancy Astor and Sir Winston Churchill.

"If this is coffee, then please bring me some tea. But if this is tea, please bring me some coffee." Abraham Lincoln.

"I think if I were a woman I'd wear coffee as a perfume." John Van Druten.

"I never laugh until I've had my coffee." Clark Gable.

"In Seattle you haven't had enough coffee until you can thread a sewing machine while it's running." Jeff Bezos.

"Sleep is a symptom of caffeine deprivation." Unknown author.

"I never drink coffee at lunch. I find it keeps me awake for the afternoon." Ronald Reagan.

"The powers of a man's mind are directly proportioned to the quantity of coffee he drinks." Sir James Mackintosh.

"Behind every successful woman is a substantial amount of coffee." Stephanie Piro.

"Decaf? No, it is dangerous to dilute my caffeine stream." Unknown author.

Aroma of Other Times

Florian's Famous Caffe in the Piazza Di San Marco, Venice,
Nineteenth Century.
From "All About Coffee" by William H. Ukers, 1922.

The legendary coffee houses are as old as coffee itself and have
served as places where people can take a break from their daily
toils and see, meet, and talk with other people. Through the last
few hundred years coffee houses have offered a convivial
meeting place, attracting people from all walks of life and
diverse interests. Artists, politicians, merchants, adventurers,
and ordinary working people have all benefitted from a cup of
freshly brewed coffee, possibly with a pastry or a light snack.

The first coffee houses were established in the Middle East. The
most famous were those of Mecca and Constantinople. Those
sites were glamorous, very stylish, and comfortable. The

15

ambience was so quiet that the customers could chat and play chess. At that time, the popularity of chess was at its peak.

It was in Venice in 1650, where the first coffee house in Europe was established. Later there were others in Marseilles, Paris, Vienna, Oxford, Cambridge and London. Coffee met with the same success in the rest of Europe. Coffee houses flourished in the Netherlands, Germany, Austria and Sweden. By the late seventeenth century coffee was enjoyed by rich and poor alike across the whole of Europe.

The golden age of London coffee houses spanned 200 years, from 1660 to 1860. Those that were located near the universities were known as *"penny universities"* because in the coffee houses commoners could improve their learning and knowledge of the world by reading newspapers, listening to speakers, and participating in discussions. Entrance cost a penny, which was deposited in a tin box that had a sign stating TIP (to insure prompt service.) A cup of coffee cost two pennies and the newspaper was free. The British coffee houses provided the best sources of information because there were bulletins on the latest political events, business and other events of daily life.

In France, coffee beans and coffee makers were imported from Turkey for the exclusive use of the nobility and the wealthy. Louis XIV so loved drinking the black elixir that he built the first greenhouse to cultivate his own coffee plants. Napoleon Bonaparte was another fan of the drink; he stated that it kept him alert. Voltaire was a prodigious coffee drinker and it is said he consumed an average of sixty cups a day! Honore de Balzac, besides being a big coffee drinker, was a connoisseur of everything related to its cultivation, processing and preparation.

As in other parts of the world, coffee houses were places where political alliances were forged and revolutions plotted. According to some historic accounts, the speech that led to the storming of the Bastille was planned at the Cafe Froy in Paris.

In 1670 coffee was brought to America and quickly became one of the most widely consumed beverages. The first coffee houses served as meeting places where, besides commenting on the news and other aspects of daily life, the Americans planned their independence. The latter took place in a coffee house in Boston known as the Green Dragon.

In the past, coffee houses served as social and cultural centres, as well as meeting places to conduct business and discuss political issues. The same is true today. While the décor, equipment, and furnishings may have undergone many changes throughout the last three hundred years, coffee houses have retained their role in bringing people together.

The Coffee Tree: Origin and Spread

Coffee is of African origin. It was discovered growing wild in the humid forests of the mountains of Ethiopia. It is said that it probably was brought to Yemen by the Arabs and cultivated there since the sixth century.

The legends differ as to the early uses for coffee. By all accounts, it was first used as food. Some Arab tribes formed balls of coffee beans and animal fat and used them as a means of subsistence as they crossed the great deserts. Later, coffee was used as a remedy to relieve some diseases. Eventually, someone came up with the idea of roasting and grinding the beans and discovered the best use for coffee—the preparation of a beverage which has since fascinated mankind.

The Arabs were the first to use coffee in their spiritual and religious practices. Later the drink spread among the royals and wealthy people who founded the first coffee houses. In the fourteenth and fifteenth centuries, coffee was deeply rooted in religion and customs of the Arabs and was declared the drink of Islam. People from other regions who tasted this drink wanted to take it home, but the Arabs did not permit the removal of the trees from their lands. They feared losing control of something they saw as their greatest treasure. But one day the inevitable happened. A Muslim pilgrim from India somehow got hold of some coffee beans that he took back to his homeland where they were successfully planted. From there the cultivation of coffee spread to Java, the Philippines, Sri Lanka (formerly Ceylon), and other Asian countries.

In the seventeenth century, coffee reached Europe and it was then that the great demand for coffee began outside the Arab world. Venetian merchants brought coffee to Europe. These beans came from Turkey where they had arrived as booty of war when the Turks invaded Arabia and its allies.

As Europeans—mainly the nobility, writers and artists—became addicted to coffee, the coffee boom spread to other regions that previously did not know of it. The main participants in this phase were Dutch and French colonialists who settled in several regions of the world.

The Dutch on some of their trips to India were able to get coffee plants. They then brought them to their new colonies, mainly to the island of Java, and with effort and luck were able to reproduce them successfully. In 1714 the Dutch gave the king of France, Louis XIV, who was a big fan of coffee, a coffee plant that had travelled from the Arab port of Mocha to Paris through the greenhouses that were in Amsterdam. The king was fascinated by the gift and immediately ordered the construction of a greenhouse where the plant was given the best care and where, for the first time, the coffee plant was the subject of scientific studies. The results were welcomed by the intellectuals of that time. This Arabica coffee plant was perhaps one of the most widespread on record, as its sprouts went to most of the legendary plantations, not only in the new world, but also in many African countries.

The spread of the coffee plant was begun by the Frenchman, Lt. Gabriel de Clieu. He first tried to convince the French authorities to give him a sapling to bring to the French colonies in the Caribbean. However, the French authorities refused to give him one, so he stole one, as others had done before.

Gabriel de Clieu travelled with his precious treasure on board a ship that was nearly wrecked in a terrible storm. Later, there were other obstacles, but finally the ship reached its destination: Martinique, where the coffee plant was cultivated with all possible care. Over time, Martinique managed to develop large plantations of coffee and, from there they exported plants to the rest of the Caribbean, Mexico, Central and South America and to some parts of Africa.

The Colours of Coffee

Imagine flying over a coffee plantation and during the flight listening to a talk about growing, harvesting and processing coffee beans. This is what you would learn:

Green Panorama

Coffee trees grow in subtropical regions where the climate and soil conditions enable the trees to flourish. They require fertile land well irrigated and drained, sufficient rain and heat, and tall trees planted to shade them. Coffee trees cannot tolerate frost and require extreme care during their lifetime.

Usually the plants are grown in nurseries and later, when they are eleven or twelve months old, are transplanted to the place where they can grow and develop. The trees take two more years before yielding their first fruits, and four years to reach full maturity. Some trees can grow up to six or eight metres but they are usually pruned to a height of two metres to facilitate harvesting of the fruit.

White Flowers and Multicolour Fruit

The coffee cycle begins when white flowers similar to jasmine appear. These flowers grow in clusters and give off a pleasant fragrance that can be picked up several miles away from the plantation. After three or four days the flowers die and the fruit starts to appear. The fruit is initially green, then turns yellow, then pink before finally becoming bright red, much like the colour and size of cherries. The coffee fruit takes six to seven months to ripen. Inside the ripened fruit are two plano-convex shaped seeds. These seeds are the coffee beans, ready for the next step of the process.

In some regions where rainfall is constant throughout the year, the plants have white flowers and green and ripe fruit simultaneously, but in other areas, where the rain alternates with a dry season, the plantations change colour as the cycle progresses. It is a marvellous spectacle to see a plantation that one day is white and another dark red.

Coffee Branches, Flowers and Fruit
From "All About Coffee" by William H. Ukers, 1922.

Encomiums and Descriptive Phrases Applied to the Plant and the Berry:

Plant

"The precious plant"
"This friendly plant"
"Mocha's happy tree"
"The gift of Heaven"
"The plant with the jessamine-like flowers"
"The most exquisite perfume of Araby the blest"

Berry

"The magic bean"
"The divine fruit"
"Fragrant berries"
"Rich, royal berry"
"Voluptuous berry"
"The precious berry"
"The healthful bean"
"The Heavenly berry"
"The marvellous berry"
"This all-healing berry"
"Yemen's fragrant berry"
"The little aromatic berry"
"Little brown Arabian berry"
"Thought-inspiring bean of Arabia"
"The smoking, ardent beans Aleppo sends"
"That wild fruit which gives so beloved a drink"

From "All About Coffee" by William H. Ukers, 1922.

Main Varieties

Many varieties of coffee are grown in different subtropical regions throughout the world. The best most widely known are Arabica and Robusta. There are great differences between the two not just morphologically, but also in taste, aroma, and especially price.

Arabica Coffee

Arabica coffee trees grow taller than Robusta trees and produce many branches that tend to cling. Arabica is grown at high altitudes, between 1350 and 2000 metres, and is sensitive to frost and vulnerable to diseases and pests. The beans are hard and thick, of great quality and highly appreciated by connoisseurs and coffee lovers. Arabica coffee is known commercially as soft and grown mainly in Colombia, Mexico, Costa Rica, Ethiopia, Guatemala, Hawaii, Jamaica, Tanzania and Yemen.

Robusta Coffee

Robusta coffee trees grow at low altitudes, between 650 and 1200 metres. They are very resilient and less susceptible to disease. Its beans are smaller and thinner, are of lower quality and contain more caffeine than Arabica beans. This variety is preferred by companies that produce instant or soluble coffee. It is cultivated mainly in Brazil, Vietnam, Dominican Republic, Ecuador, Haiti, India, Peru, Venezuela and Kenya.

Harvesting and Processing

The quantity and quality of coffee beans obtained from the same plant can vary from harvest to harvest. There are no two identical crops as the coffee tree can be affected by changes in climate and soil conditions and procedures used in harvesting.

In coffee-growing regions, harvesting the coffee fruit involves everyone in the community, young and old, male and female. From the air, the plantation appears to be full of voracious ants picking the fruits as they mature, and going over the trees again and again until there are no red berries left. This manual procedure provides quality coffee and is an important factor in its flavour. Most of the Arabica coffee producers use this harvesting procedure.

In recent years, machines have appeared to collect the beans selectively. The procedure is simple and consists of shaking the coffee tree so the ripe fruit falls off, leaving the green fruits for the next time the harvester passes. This process is not commonly used in traditional plantations where the owners prefer to pay for the manual harvesting of the fruit. In general, in coffee-producing countries, labor is cheap.

Once harvested, the fruit is processed by one of two methods: the dry or the wet (or *"washed"*, as it is sometimes called).

Dry Method

The dry method is the oldest and cheapest, and it is used in areas where fresh, clean water is scarce. In Brazil, 90% of plantations apply this method to pulp and clean their coffee beans. It involves strewing the fruits over outside brick or concrete surfaces where they can be dried naturally by the sun. The fruits are turned frequently so that drying is even. Once their skin is wrinkled, it comes off easily, as does the flesh that protects the beans. The latter can be done manually or by pulping machines that facilitate the task. Finally comes the cleaning phase where any impurities are removed before the beans get packed in 60 kilo bags for shipping.

Wet Method

The wet or washing process is more complicated than the dry process. After the coffee berries have been harvested, it is necessary to remove their coating. This is done by carefully removing the coating layer by layer. A pulping machine is used to remove the peel and pulp, but, as the seeds are still covered with a sticky substance, they are soaked in water to ferment. Fermentation enzymes are responsible for cleaning the seeds from this sticky substance. Next, the beans are washed and dried, either using an industrial dryer or the sun. Finally, a hulling machine is used to remove the last layer, which is known as parchment.

The process concludes with the cleaning and sorting of the beans, which at this stage are called golden or green coffee. Cleaning consists mainly of removing defective beans, garbage and other foreign elements. When it comes to very fine beans like Arabica, this inspection is performed up to three times.

Classification

Quality control standards for coffee beans vary from country to country. The most common quality standards assess the quality of the beans, their size, flavour, aroma and their blending qualities, as well as the place of origin and the altitude at which they were harvested and processed. There is another classification criterion based on the number of imperfections of the beans per kilogram. These imperfections can include broken or defective beans, stones, straw and other foreign materials.

Once the above steps are completed, the green coffee is put up for sale on the international market. The coffee beans are sold directly in the country of origin or through intermediaries or brokers who have the knowledge required to know what kind of beans they are buying and whether the beans are suitable to make the blends asked for by their customers.

Typical coffee scene in Costa Rica.

From "All About Coffee" by William H. Ukers, 1922.

Fair Trade Coffee

As is well known, the poorest countries produce the most coffee and this is consumed by the richer countries that pay a lot of money for the drink and too little for the green beans. This is why coffee farmers remain poor despite their hard work.

Fair Trade was introduced by several coffee consumer countries, the Netherlands, Germany and the United States among others, more than thirty years ago to reduce poverty. The concept looks simple: "Coffee is a big business. We purchase green beans at a low price and make lots of money with them. Let's pay more to the coffee producers so they can improve their quality of life and we can continue having our cup of coffee." But it is a really complicated matter. In order to get the certification of Fair Trade, the farmers have to be members of a democratically run cooperative; they cannot hire child labour; they have to comply with the restrictions on the use of herbicides and pesticides, and many more rules. Even with the certification, the farmers cannot sell all their production at Fair Trade prices; they are allowed to sell only a small percentage of the crops as Fair Trade certified and the rest at regular world prices. Not all the crops are of the same quality, so due to this restriction the farmers opt for selling the low quality part of the crops at Fair Trade price and the best part and their organic grown coffee at world prices as specialty coffee.

Despite the good intentions with which Fair Trade was created, it has not had the expected results until now. But we understand that change takes a long time and some day, maybe in the near future, coffee farmers will have a better quality of life and consumers of Fair Trade certified coffee will receive good quality beans.

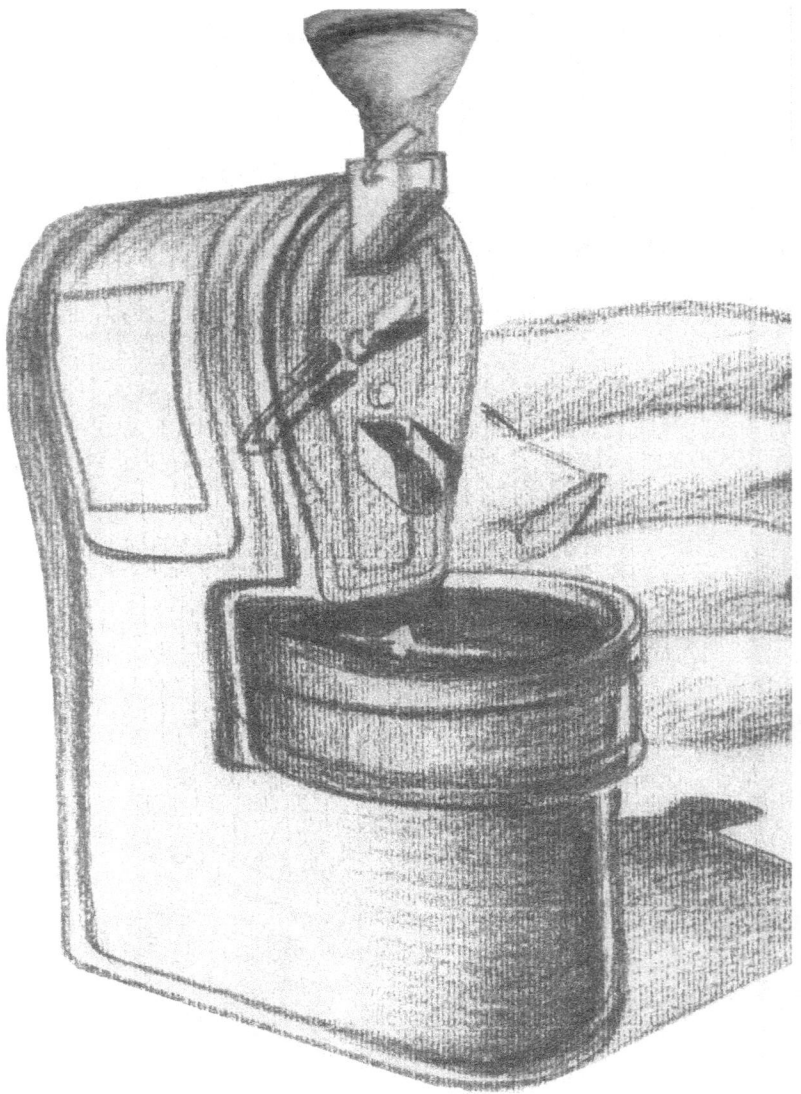

Before the First Sip

Before you can enjoy your cup of coffee, green beans have to go through a few more steps. First, they must be roasted to bring out their full flavour and aroma. Once they are roasted, coffee beans can be blended with other roasted beans to produce a full-bodied, aromatic taste. Finally the beans have to be ground to different consistencies to suit the different types of coffee makers.

Roasting

The green bean has no smell or flavour of coffee. It has the ability to develop these qualities but it needs to go through a heating process to do so. When the heat of the roaster forces the moisture out, it forms drops of a fragrant, volatile oil, and it is at this stage that the green beans smell and taste like coffee.

In theory, roasting coffee is not a difficult job. The beans must be heated to a certain temperature and for a certain time depending on the degree of roasting desired, and must be kept in motion in order to get an even roast and to prevent them from burning.

Easy in theory, but in reality you need to know what happens to the beans at each stage of the process. Roasting requires training, skill, experience and inspiration. Good roasters can control the flavours they want to enhance and those they want to hide. Roasting coffee is an art that requires study, practice and quality equipment.

Coffee roasters who sell gourmet coffee use simple equipment consisting of a rotating drum, a heat source, and a tank to cool the beans. The important thing here is that they roast the beans in small batches, controlling the process with skill and experience to ensure that the aroma and colour fully develop.

By controlling the roasting process, roasters can produce coffee beans that range in colour from a very light brown to a very dark one. There are five degrees of roasting. Each is given a different name in different countries and varies in taste, aroma and appearance. The names that appear here are the most common.

The light roast produces beans with a dry appearance, and as its name indicates, is light in colour and taste. With light roasting, the full oils do not completely emerge. Known as *Cinnamon*, *New England*, or plain *Light Roast* in North America, this grade of roasting has a mild coffee flavour and a characteristic acidic taste.

Medium roasted coffee also has a dry surface and is often called *Regular, American or Medium*. It has a full-coffee flavour and a touch of acidity, but is richer and sweeter than light roast.

The next degree of roasting is the dark light. It is a little darker than the previous roast and with a little oil on the surface. It is known as *Light French, Viennese, City, Full City or Espresso Light*. Its taste is bitter sweet and less acidic than the other roasts.

The dark roast has a shiny, oily surface. It goes by the names of *Italian, Espresso, European, French, Continental* or *Dark*. It has a definite sweet-sour taste and it is not acidic.

Coffee Tasting

A good way to determine the quality of the beans is to try them. Purchasing experts of fine beans taste coffee looking for aroma, acidity, body and flavour of each sample and decide which to buy. The experts know there can be real differences between coffee beans even when they come from the same country or region. Anyone interested in coffees should learn to distinguish between them by sensitizing his or her palate to the subtleties of flavour, aroma, acidity, and body.

Aroma is the first feature detected in coffee. The smell indicates the freshness and type of coffee. This quality is responsible for its popularity and appeal.

Body is related to the sense of consistency and texture created in the mouth by coffee. Basically, this quality refers to the density of the drink, and it is detected through the palate.

Acidity must not be mistaken with a bitter or sour taste. The term is used to describe the pungent flavour that gives life to coffee.

Finally, flavour is the most important quality and it is the most difficult one to describe because it is the combination of the three qualities above. The flavour allows us to detect any defect in the coffee beans, as well as in the roasting and handling they undergo before reaching the customer. For example, flavour tells us if the beans were burned when they were roasted, if it has a stale taste due to improper storage, or if the beans are old.

Blending Coffee

A blend is a combination of coffee beans that have come from either different countries or different roasting processes. Blends offer more variety and delicacy of flavours than the ones available from a single source. For example, by mixing coffee whose main characteristic is aroma with one whose flavour and body dominate, we can get a great cup of coffee.

There are some exceptional coffees that do not need to be blended because they have all the characteristics desirable in a good coffee. It is a sensory pleasure to enjoy them on their own.

You can make your own blends based on taste. You should consider the qualities you prefer in coffee and mix different coffees to get them. If you have a favourite coffee but it lacks a particular taste, combine it with a coffee that has that taste.

Grinding Coffee

In order to extract all the flavour of roasted coffee, it must be ground. The grind will depend on the method used to brew coffee.

The regular or coarse grind is best suited for the methods in which the coffee particles are in contact with water for six to eight minutes, as with the percolator.

The middle ground is for methods that take four to six minutes, as in the filter coffee maker and French press.

The fine grind is appropriate for methods that take less than a minute, like espresso.

Roasted coffee is well preserved for up to two weeks, but if it is ground it breaks down faster because the delicate oils when exposed to air immediately begin to evaporate. An airtight container helps but not much, so, the best way to preserve coffee is to keep the whole beans until they are ready to be used, and only then, should they be ground. Grinding coffee does not take long if you have the right appliance. Currently, there are several types of easy-to-use manual and electric coffee grinders on the market.

The most common coffee grinder is electric with blades. The time required to produce different degrees of grinding in one of these is approximately:

Time	Grinding	Coffee Maker
10 seconds	coarse	Percolator
15 seconds	medium	Automatic Drip
30 seconds	fine	Espresso

Times above may vary depending on the kind of coffee grinder you use. Carefully read the operating instructions before you grind your coffee.

Packaging and Preservation

Green coffee beans can be kept in good condition for many years. Once they are roasted they lose their flavour in about two weeks and, after they are ground, deterioration begins within hours. After roasting, coffee is packaged in different ways, depending on its destination.

Small roasters use paper or plastic bags. Their product does not need to be stored for a long time because it is sold the same day it is roasted.

Commercial coffees are packaged in vacuum bags or cans that can be stored for several months in warehouses and on supermarket shelves. Vacuum packaging delays the breakdown of coffee since it eliminates most of the air inside the bag or can. Roasted coffee expels carbon dioxide for some time after being roasted. If freshly roasted coffee is packed immediately, the cans would swell and the bags would break because of the gas formed inside. For that reason, coffee is left to stand in open tanks prior to being packaged. Vacuum-packed coffee, therefore, is not as fresh as it should be.

Exhaust Valve

To ensure that coffee reaches consumers in a fresher state, coffee producers have devised a valve for their vacuum-packed bags. The valve enables the carbon dioxide to escape without letting the air into the bag, operating on the principle of pressure differences. When the pressure inside the bag is greater than the external pressure, it opens, releasing the gases; when the pressures are equal, it closes. Once the bag is open for use, the valve ceases to have a function.

To keep coffee fresh, you should store it in tightly sealed containers. In this way, the coffee oils do not evaporate, and the coffee retains its aroma and flavour.

Caffeinated or Decaffeinated

"Caffeine is not a drug, it is a vitamin"
Unknown author.

When coffee is consumed in moderation it stimulates our entire nervous system, thereby increasing our productivity, sensory functions, and mental processes.

Caffeine is an alkaloid found naturally in coffee, tea, cocoa and some other plants. Caffeine is habit forming and it is feared that its excessive consumption can cause some diseases, although there is no medical evidence to prove so at present.

If you want to avoid using caffeine, there is an alternative: decaffeinated coffee. It contains only 3% of the caffeine in untreated coffee. The coffee flavour is not affected by decaffeination, since caffeine lacks aroma and flavour. The best decaffeinated coffees, freshly roasted and ground and carefully prepared, taste as good as standard coffees. Only when they are compared at the same time will a slight difference be noticed. Unfortunately, there is not a large variety of decaffeinated coffees, but you can make a low-caffeine blend by combining your favourite coffee with a decaffeinated coffee.

If you lined all the walls of your home with coffee motifs as posters, photos, pictures, rugs, paintings, etc.

If your eyes are in lunar orbit

If your wife finds out that you sleep with your eyes open

Be careful ... you are consuming too much caffeine.

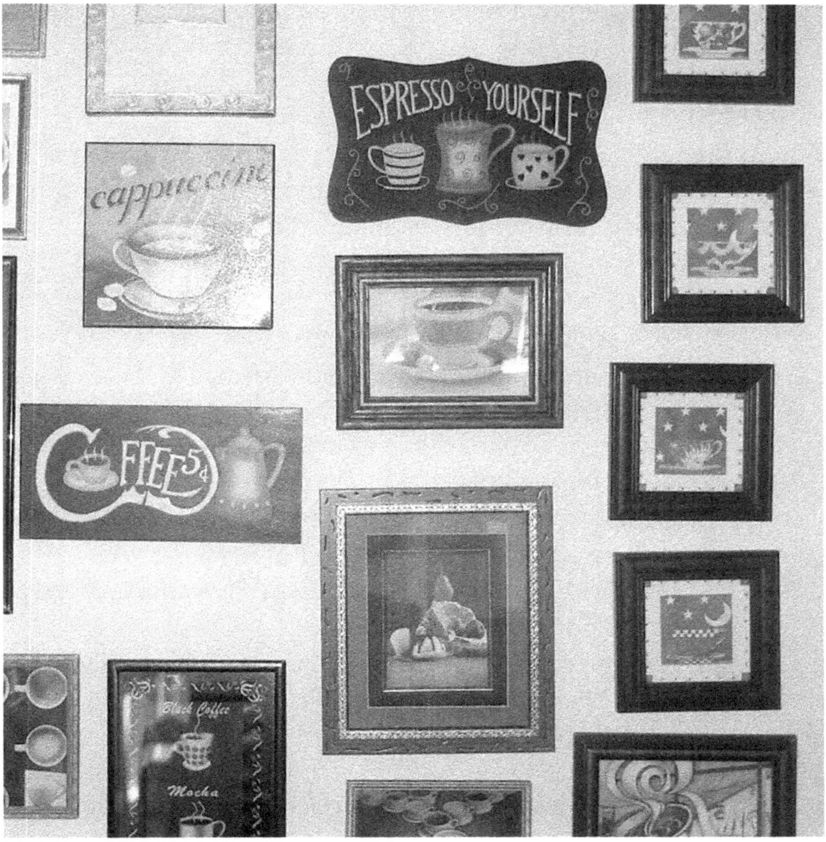
ESPRESSO YOURSELF
Black Coffee
Mocha

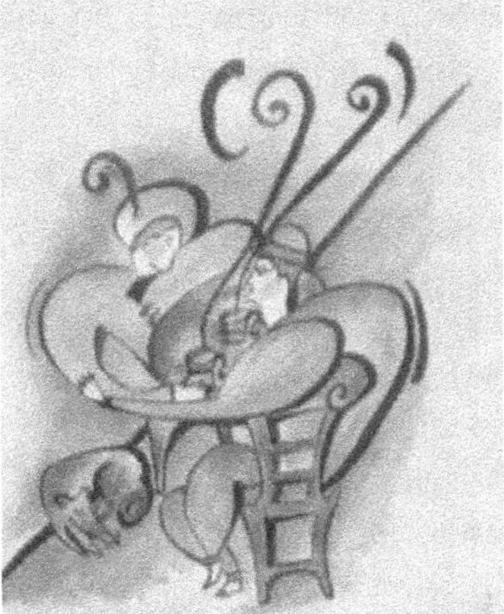

Fresh Coffee

To prepare a delicious cup of coffee at home, you must use the best beans available, the proper coffee maker and then follow some specific instructions, as detailed below:

- Use good quality coffee beans.
- The water should be clean and fresh. Use bottled water or filtered water because it has no odour or taste that can ruin your coffee. Remember that water is about 98% of every cup of coffee.
- Grind the coffee just before brewing it. The grind should be appropriate for the method of brewing you use. If the grind is too coarse the coffee will be watery; if the grind is too fine, it will be bitter.
- Use the right amount of coffee. Experts recommend using the right proportion of coffee to water: 2 tablespoons (10 grams) of ground coffee for every 6 ounces (180 ml.) of water. This proportion can be adjusted according to your taste. One tablespoon for each cup of water is a good starting point. Experiment and decide on your own preference.
- Always preheat your cup to keep your coffee hot longer.
- Stir the coffee with a spoon before serving it so the flavour is even throughout the pot.
- Serve coffee immediately after brewing it, or put it in a thermos to keep it warm. Never reheat coffee or reuse the beans.
- Do not leave the coffee pot on the hotplate of the coffee maker for over 30 minutes. After that time, you will have a concentrated drink which is bitter and odourless.
- Clean your coffee maker so that flavours are not added to your next cup of coffee.

- Do not forget that nothing is more inviting than a freshly brewed coffee for its well defined flavour. Smell the aroma before taking the first sip from a cup of coffee.
- Always use china cups to serve your coffee. They keep the coffee temperature longer. In glass and plastic cups coffee cools rapidly.

Preparation Procedures

Brewing methods vary and change not only as people's tastes change but also as new coffee-making appliances come on the market. Since coffee was adopted as a drink, all kinds of coffee makers have been invented for its preparation. They range from a modest bowl of water and a heat source to the most sophisticated coffee maker for which you just need to press a button to get a steaming cup of coffee.

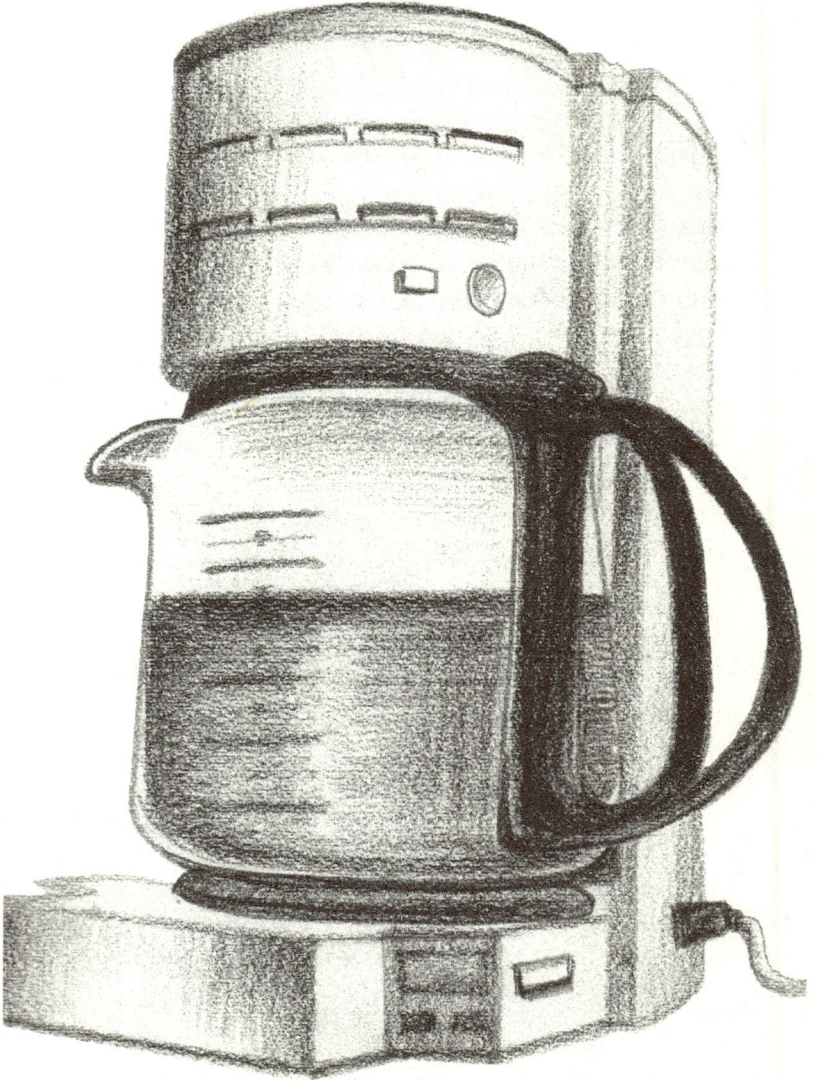

The Filter or Drip Method

The filter or drip method is the most commonly used today. It consists basically of passing boiling water through ground coffee in a filter. A number of models of electric coffee makers are based on this principle.

The filter coffee maker usually consists of a water tank and a system for boiling the water, a glass pot, its cover and a filter basket. These units operate as follows: water is boiled in the water tank then it drips over the coffee grounds into the glass pot on the hot plate below.

To make coffee in a filter coffee machine, you just have to put the number of cups of cold water needed in the tank, place the filter in the filter basket, put one tablespoon of medium ground coffee for each cup of water into the filter, activate the coffee maker, and your coffee will be ready in less than ten minutes.

This method is convenient, quick and easy. It is not only popular at home, but also in offices. The filter coffee maker was developed to replace the percolator.

Some people whose palate is very sensitive find that paper coffee filters have a drawback: they can transmit paper flavour to the coffee. Fortunately, coffee drinkers can purchase filters that have been bleached with chlorine oxygen. There are also gold-plated filters (actually, they are made from steel and coated with a light gold plating) on the market. They are expensive but last a long time. They do not have to be replaced every time you want to make a fresh pot of coffee, but perhaps most importantly of all, they do not destroy any essential oils the way many paper filters do.

French Press

The French press, as the name implies, gives a European touch to the preparation of coffee.

The press is one of the best ways to brew coffee. It is preferred by many Europeans and it has recently gained wide acceptance in the United States and other countries. These coffee makers are now available not only in specialty shops, but also in a number of department stores.

The French press consists of a cylindrical glass jar with a metal rod running through the centre of the lid. This rod has a ball handle on top and a flat filter that fits perfectly into the jar, at the bottom. This device moves up and down inside the jar, much like a plunger.

To make coffee in a French press, put the necessary amount of medium ground coffee into the jar, pour in boiling water and put the lid on. The rod should be up. Let it stand for 4 minutes and push the rod to the bottom of the jar. In this way the coffee is filtered, leaving the coffee grounds at the bottom, separated from the drink. The resulting coffee is dense and tastes delicious and much better, according to some fans of this method, than the one obtained with a coffee machine.

Turkish Coffee

This method originated in the Middle East, and it is still used by Turks, Arabs and Greeks. This is the way flavour was extracted from coffee beans in the beginning. The process is simple and the resulting drink is strong and thick.

It uses a copper or brass pot called an ibrik and for each cup of coffee you want to prepare, you use two teaspoons of dark roasted and finely ground coffee, two teaspoons of sugar and 1/4 cup cold water.

With the Turkish method you can make several cups at once, but try not to fill the ibrik more than halfway. Place the ibrik on the stove until the water boils and the foam rises to the top. Remove from the heat for the foam to go down. Repeat this procedure two more times and serve the coffee in small cups with a little foam on top. Allow it to sit and then enjoy your coffee.

The Turkish method leaves sediment of coffee grounds in the bottom of your cup and for that reason is used by clairvoyants or fortune tellers to "read" their customer's future.

47

Traditional Method

The traditional method was the one used by most people in the west before the advent of modern coffee makers. This method involves boiling water in a container, then removing it from the heat source before adding a tablespoon of coarse ground coffee per cup of water. The coffee is then stirred and returned to the fire, but this time on a very low heat for 3 to 5 minutes, without letting it boil. When it is ready it is strained before being served. The quality of the drink depends on the degree of grinding, the care taken to measure the amounts of water and coffee, and the timing.

The traditional method is very popular in Mexico where it is called *café de olla*. Water with some brown sugar is boiled for three minutes in a classic clay pot called an *olla*. A few sticks of cinnamon and the coffee are added after the water has finished boiling. If you add tequila, mezcal or some other spirit to *café de olla*, you get *café con piquete*.

An interesting variation of the traditional method is the sock method. Boil a specified amount of water and then soak a clean sock (you can use a cheesecloth bag instead) with a measured tablespoon of coarsely ground coffee per cup of water in it. Leave the pot to simmer on low heat until the coffee has a good colour. Remove the sock and serve the coffee.

Percolator

The percolator method fills a room with the delicious aroma of freshly brewed coffee. Delicious! But the smell should remain in the coffee and not be lost to the environment. Percolation is not the best way to brew coffee because it violates several basic rules for obtaining a good cup. The most important of them is that the drink being prepared passes over and over the coffee grounds and by doing this the bitter taste of coffee is released along with the good taste.

The percolator has a basket filter and a central tube inside. When the water boils, it goes up through the tube and passes through the ground coffee contained in the filter. Then it falls and mixes with the water that continues boiling, and goes up again through the tube and repeats this again and again during the entire cycle, defying the rule that the drink should not boil. The percolator is still used in some homes and especially in certain offices, where fresh coffee tastes good in the morning, but hours later that coffee tastes very unpleasant.

Just Press the Button

Coffee capsules are becoming more and more popular. They are used in one-cup coffee makers.

The coffee is dispensed and packaged in aluminium or plastic capsules. The manufacturers of these capsules also sell the coffee makers that use coffee capsules. These coffee makers brew one cup of coffee at a time.

The downside of this new brewing process is that it is expensive and adds to landfill waste.

Coffee Drinks

Viennese Coffee

Drink this traditional beverage along with a Viennese Sacher Torte, the most famous chocolate cake. The recipe can be found on page 89.

1/2 cup of coffee
1/2 cup of hot milk with foam
Sugar to taste

Combine coffee with milk and sweeten to taste.

Coffee with Vanilla and Chocolate
A unique and irresistible taste.

1 cup of coffee
1 tablespoon chocolate syrup
1/4 teaspoon vanilla
1/4 cup whipped cream

Mix vanilla and chocolate syrup with coffee. Garnish with whipped cream.

Hawaiian Coffee

Try something magical.

1/2 cup of coffee
1/2 cup milk
2 tablespoons shredded coconut

Put the milk and 1 tablespoon of coconut in a small saucepan simmer for 3 minutes, stirring occasionally. Strain the milk. Put the remaining tablespoon of coconut in a pan and toast lightly for 5 minutes. Add milk to hot coffee and sprinkle with toasted coconut.

Liquor Coffee Drinks

Mixing coffee with the aroma of liquor has always been a great idea.

The following is a list of spirits that combine well with coffee: Kahlua, Grand Marnier, cognac, whiskey, Amaretto, vodka, Drambuie, rum.

The result of this marriage is a variety of delicious recipes.

Irish coffee and Brulot coffee are classic drinks. They top the list of recipes that are prepared with coffee and liquor as basic ingredients. They are served before, with or after dessert; in fact some of these drinks are considered as desserts.

Here are some tips on how to get the best liquor coffee drinks:
- Preheat your cups and glasses with hot water.
- Add the brewed coffee.
- Add sugar, flavouring and garnish as desired.

Irish Coffee

Classic coffee for a winter afternoon.

1 cup of coffee
1 oz. Irish whiskey
1 teaspoon sugar
Whipped cream

Mix coffee, whiskey and sugar. Garnish with whipped cream.

Brulot Coffee

Also called the Devil's coffee.

1 cup extra-strong coffee
1 tablespoon brown sugar
2 cloves
1 piece of orange peel
1 piece of lemon peel
1 oz. brandy

Heat the brandy, sugar, cloves and orange and lemon peel to simmer, stirring constantly to dissolve sugar. When the brandy is hot and has a strong aroma, remove from the heat. Serve coffee in a cup. Pour the brandy carefully (with a spoon) on coffee to float. Pass a lit match over the cup to light the liquor. To extinguish the flame stir with a spoon after a few seconds.

Coffee with Kahlua

This drink is great to enjoy with friends and family.

3/4 cup of coffee
1/4 cup whipped cream
1 oz. Kahlua
Sweetened cocoa powder

Mix the coffee with Kahlua. Garnish with whipped cream and sprinkle with cocoa powder.

Orange Coffee

Delicious!

3/4 cup of coffee
1 oz. orange liqueur
1/4 cup whipping cream
1 tablespoon confectioner's sugar
1/2 teaspoon orange zest
1 orange slice for garnish

Beat cream with confectioner's sugar until stiff peaks form. Add the orange zest and mix well. Serve coffee in a glass cup. Add liquor and a good portion of whipped cream. Place the slice of orange on the rim of the cup.

Tropical Coffee
A lovely combination.

2/3 cup of coffee
2 tablespoons Grand Marnier
1 oz. rum
Whipped cream
Shredded coconut
Orange zest
Lemon zest
Brown sugar to taste

Serve liquor in a glass cup. Add coffee and brown sugar and mix well. Garnish with whipped cream, grated coconut and a little orange and lemon zest.

Mocha with Rum
Reminiscent of a sugar cane plantation.

1/2 cup of coffee
1/2 cup hot milk
2 tablespoons chocolate syrup
1/8 teaspoon ground cinnamon
1 pinch of salt
1 tablespoon chocolate chips
1 oz. rum
Whipped cream

Combine chocolate syrup and coffee. Add pinch of salt and cinnamon. Stir well. Place milk in blender for a few seconds to form a lather. Add it to coffee with 2 tablespoons of rum. Mix well and garnish with whipped cream and some chocolate chips.

Rum Summer Cocktail

1/4 cup of fresh coffee
1/4 cup of cocoa liquor
2 oz. dark rum
Ice cubes

Mix in shaker and serve strained in a cocktail glass.

"Making my own espresso at home is a little extra work, but I don't mind."

Espresso

This delightful and romantic beverage deserves a separate chapter. Espresso is considered by coffee lovers as *"The Cognac of coffee"* and *"a drink for gourmets"* for its bitter-sweet flavour and creamy consistency, features not found in other types of coffee.

Espresso is made by a unique process that extracts the "soul" of coffee using pressure. A combination of steam and boiling water is passed under pressure through a small amount of coffee contained in a filter, yielding a dark-bodied drink with a thin layer of creamy foam on top.

According to some coffee aficionados, espresso comes from the Italian word meaning *faster*, but others believe it comes from the French word *express*, which means *explicit*. The origin of the word is obscure, which probably contributes to the drink's mysterious aura. Espresso has been described as the *"soul of coffee"*.

Italians maintain that real espresso is prepared by passing 25 ml. of water at a temperature between 88°C and 92°C at a pressure of 9 atmospheres through 6 or 7 grams of finely ground coffee for 25 seconds. They use four M factors to prepare their perfect espresso: Miscela (Mixing), Macinacione (Grinding), Macchina (Machine) and Mano (Hand). The mixing involves selecting the best roasted coffee beans. The grinding must produce a fine powdery texture. Machine and hand refer to the espresso machine and its skilled operator. When all four M factors are precisely controlled, you obtain the perfect beverage.

A person who prepares and serves these beverages in cafes and espresso bars is known by the name of *"barista"*. This term originated in Italy and from there it went to the U.S. and the rest of the world. The barista must complete studies and training covering the general aspects of different types of coffee, the use and management of coffee, and beverage preparation.

Espresso Coffee Makers

Italy has the highest espresso consumption in the world. It also has the distinction of being the place where espresso coffee makers have evolved.

There are two types of home espresso makers: the stove top espresso maker and the electric espresso maker. The first one heats the water in the lower chamber until it reaches the required pressure to power it up through the filter containing the coffee grounds, thereby extracting their rich aroma and flavour. Some of these coffee makers have a steam valve that is used to prepare milk for cappuccinos. The other alternative is an electric coffee maker. There are several brands on the market and the price depends on the features offered by each.

If you plan to buy an electric espresso machine, check its level of power, because if it is not powerful enough, you will be frustrated trying to produce milk foam for cappuccinos. We suggest buying an automatic pump espresso machine of at least 750 watts.

Possibly you have the best espresso machine in the market, but if you do not fully understand the process for making espresso, the results can be disastrous. In the following pages, you will find a practical guide for making espresso the way the best barista does. Have fun following these simple steps, and practise them as often as necessary so that you can be successful in preparing this aromatic and delicious drink.

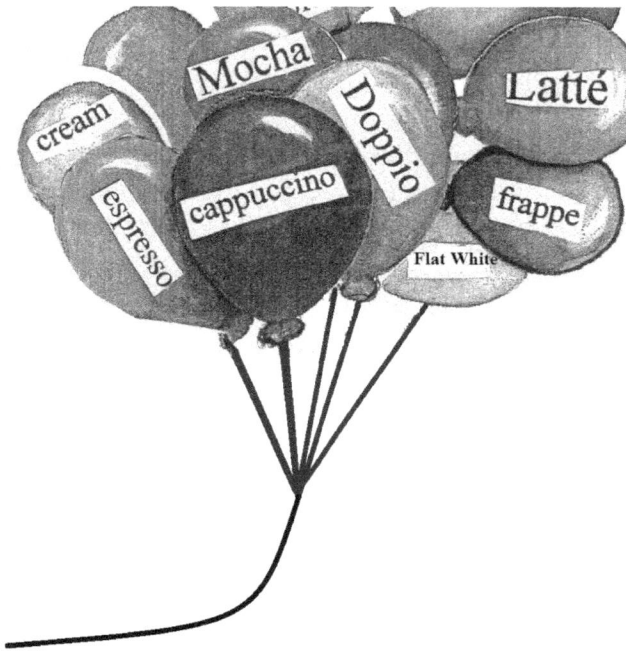

Preparing Espresso at Home

What is required:

The Coffee

The process of making espresso brings out the flavourful acids of the coffee beans. For this reason, dark roasted beans are the preferred choice for making espresso.

Coffee beans should be ground to a fine texture, similar to coarsely ground pepper. Keeping that in mind, you need to grind ½ cup of quality, recently dark roasted coffee beans. Stir it with a spoon to make sure the coffee is ground to a uniform texture. You will use this to learn to make espresso.

The cups

Use the special small espresso cups, known by the name of *demitasse*. Cappuccino and latté are served in normal size cups.

A measuring glass

To determine the amount of espresso to prepare, you need a 2-ounce glass which is equivalent to 60 millilitres. These small glasses known as *shot glasses* are used to prepare alcoholic drinks. This is the measure used in the recipes in this book.

A measuring spoon

If the coffee maker did not come with one, use a tablespoon measure.

The Water

Although it has been already mentioned, it is worth noting that water is an important ingredient in the preparation of coffee. If the tap water is not good in the place where you live, use bottled water.

Procedure

Espresso Machine

- Before you prepare the first espresso, read the manufacturer's instructions carefully.

- Fill the machine's water tank with fresh water.

- Run the machine without coffee, just to fill the cup and the measuring glass with hot water since the amount of espresso will be small and it will cool in a moment in a cold cup. Keep the hot water in the cup until ready to serve the espresso.

- Put 1 ½ tablespoons of espresso ground coffee in the filter and compress it. Remove any coffee particles from the edge of the filter to prevent steam leakage. Place the filter on the machine and the measuring glass underneath.

- Press the water button, let it run for 20 to 25 seconds and turn off the machine. You should get 1 ½ ounces of espresso in that time.

- Watch the quality of your espresso. First smell it. The scent should be intense. Observe the *"crema"*; it should be an extremely thin foam with a colour varying from a light brown to a dark gold. Sprinkle a few grains of sugar on it. If the grains float before sinking, you have achieved success in preparing espresso.

- Clean your machine after each use. A machine that has not been properly cleaned can ruin the next cup of espresso prepared in it.

Cappuccino Froth

Your espresso machine can provide the steam you need to produce the foam of your cappuccino, latté or mocha.

When milk is heated with steam, proteins are altered in a different way than when it is heated directly on the stove. The flavour acquired when heated with steam is delicious.

Heating the milk with steam is easy. All you have to do is submerge the steam pipe in a container with milk and open the steam valve, leaving it open until the milk reaches the desired temperature.

Foaming is more complicated. For optimum results, you need cold skim milk. With cold milk, froth is obtained more easily, so do not heat the milk first; foam it and then heat it. Foam can be obtained with any milk, but with skim milk it is easier to achieve.

You will need a small stainless steel cylinder-shaped container. The size of the container matters because the steam from your espresso machine is enough to produce foam only for 1 or 1 1/2 cups of milk. Use a container that is not too deep, because to heat the milk you will need to submerge the steam pipe to the bottom and it is not very long. Milk will double or triple its volume in this process. Be careful not to overfill your container as you might get some scalding spills and splashes!

Submerge the steam nozzle into a container with water and turn on the steam valve. This is to remove water that may have accumulated in the tube. Once the steam starts coming out, close the valve and replace the container of water with one of milk and open the valve completely to get the maximum steam pressure. As soon as you open the valve, lower the container so that the tip of the tube is just under the surface of the milk. If it remains above the surface, it can splatter milk everywhere and form very large bubbles that will quickly disappear. Keeping the tube just below the surface of the milk will allow air to be pushed into the milk by the power of steam, creating tiny bubbles that accumulate on the surface becoming foam.

Once you have a nice foam, you are ready to move on to the recipe section and apply what you have learned so far.

Latté Art

Some baristas are able to make art such as drawings of hearts, leaves, female faces and other figures on latté foam. This is accomplished by the movement of the wrist when pouring the milk foam into the coffee. It takes much practice and patience to master this art.

There are latté art competitions around the world. One of the most important is the World Latté Art Championship. It is organized several times a year in different cities.

The World Latté Art Championship challenges the baristas to show off their artistic soul. It is a delight for the coffee lovers to watch the creation of hundreds of different patterns and designs.

Preparing Espresso in a Stove Top Espresso Maker

Although this procedure does not yield the same results as an automatic pump espresso machine, the price and ease of purchase in major department stores make it attractive.

To make a delicious cup of espresso using a stove-top espresso maker – also called *moka express* – you need to follow the next steps:

- Unscrew the top of the espresso maker.
- Remove the filter and fill the bottom part with cold water to the level indicated.
- Fill the filter almost to the top with dark roasted finely ground coffee. If you do not use the right amount, you will get a drink of poor quality.
- Set the filter in place.
- Adjust the top to the base and put the espresso maker on the stove over medium heat.
- When you hear the coffee bubbling, remove it from heat. When the water boils, the pressure will make it go up and pass through the filter containing the coffee and now espresso is in the top part of the espresso maker ready to be served.
- Serve espresso in demitasses.

Some fans of the drink usually add sugar to balance the strong flavour. It can also be served with a bit of lemon peel or a thin slice of lemon on the side. This variation is called espresso Romano.

Some espresso drinkers like to add a dash of cinnamon or nutmeg, or a few drops of vanilla to enhance the flavour.

To prepare a cappuccino or latté, froth the milk using a battery operated or a manual milk frother. Coffee frothers are available online, in kitchen supplies stores, and in department stores.

Sunday Morning Coffee

Relaxed dragons like Kypogo and Karmela tend to enjoy their morning coffee. In summer they enjoy it on their spacious deck and in winter they have it in their studio.

On this particular Sunday morning, Kypogo wanted his wife to prepare a cappuccino, but they don't have an espresso machine at home. And so he asked his wife to forget this idea.

"Don't worry my love, I know how to prepare a delicious cappuccino with a stove top espresso maker and a milk frother", said Karmela. "She must have read it on the Internet", thought Kypogo.

Karmela first ground enough fresh coffee beans for two cups and put them into the filter and added fresh water into the bottom part of the espresso maker. In a few minutes she had fresh espresso. Then she heated the milk for one minute, frothed it and prepared a delicious cappuccino. She didn't forget to warm the mugs before pouring the hot milk and the espresso.

They then went to their ritual place, sipped their cappuccinos and discussed the news of the day.

This is how to prepare cappuccino without an espresso machine:

- Heat the milk in a saucepan on the stove until just before boiling.
- Place the whisking end of the frother just barely under the surface of the hot milk.
- Turn the frother on and move the whisk around the surface of the milk. The movement will create foam on the top of the milk. Turn the frother off when you get about 1/2 inch of thick foam.
- Rinse the frother under warm running water to thoroughly clean it. Run the frother for a few seconds outside the water, the air will dry it.
- Pour enough milk in a hot mug to fill it to one third.
- Pour espresso on top of the milk to about two thirds of the mug. Pour it slowly and it won't mix with the milk.
- Place milk foam on top and add a little cinnamon powder on top.
- Add sugar if desired.

Electric Milk Frother   Manual Milk Frother

Espresso Drinks

Enjoy the pleasure of dark roasted espresso, rich and creamy cappuccino and the delicious cafe mocha in this collection of recipes. All of them have been tested and adapted for this publication and only the best and the easiest to prepare were selected. The recipes are divided into two categories:

Espresso alone   Espresso with milk

Most people's palate leans more to espresso drinks with milk, like cappuccino, but it is also worth trying the espresso alone.

All drinks in this section begin with a basic espresso and are served in *demitasse* cups. Sweeten them to taste. Feel free to experiment all you want. Vary the amount of espresso or other ingredients, or add flavour extracts or liqueurs.

Espresso Hot Drinks

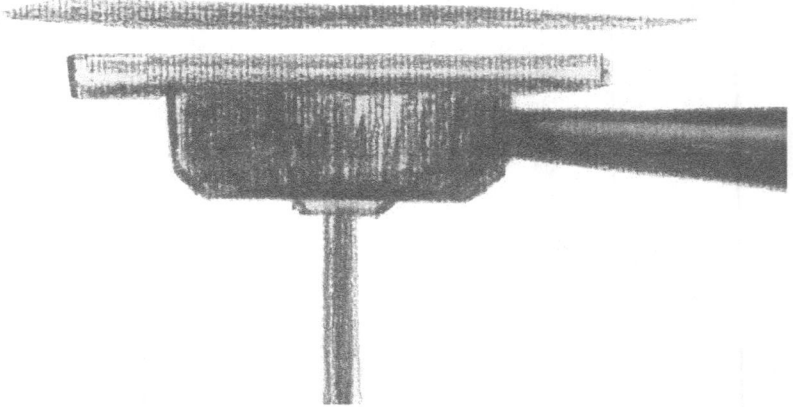

Espresso (A single shot of espresso)

2 oz. espresso
Sugar to taste

Serve espresso in a demitasse with sugar to taste.

Doppio (Double Espresso)

4 oz. espresso
Sugar to taste

Serve espresso in a demitasse with sugar to taste.

Espresso with Panna

2 oz. espresso
Whipped cream

Serve espresso and garnish with a dollop of whipped cream.

Espresso Borgia

2 oz. espresso
Whipped cream
Orange zest

Serve espresso. Garnish with a dollop of whipped cream and orange zest.

Espresso Macchiato Borgia

2 oz. espresso
2 teaspoons milk foam
Orange zest

Serve espresso in a demitasse and garnish with foamed milk and orange zest.

Espresso Romano

2 oz. espresso
1 small piece of lemon peel

Serve espresso in a demitasse and let the lemon peel float on it.

Espresso Cold Drinks

Cold Espresso Maple

4 oz. espresso
2 teaspoons maple syrup
Ice cubes
Whipped cream

Dissolve the maple syrup in the espresso. Serve over ice cubes and garnish with whipped cream.

Espresso Frappe

12 oz. cold espresso
3 cups chopped or crushed ice
Sugar to taste
1/2 lemon + 3 lemon slices

Blend the espresso, sugar and ice in an electric blender. Rub the rims of the glasses with lemon and frost them with sugar. Pour the espresso frappe in the glasses and garnish with a slice of lemon on the rim.

Espresso Drinks with Milk

Classic Cappuccino
More than a simple cup of coffee.

4 oz. espresso
4 oz. steamed milk
4 oz. milk foam
Cinnamon, nutmeg or cocoa

Serve espresso combined with the milk and topped with foam.
Sprinkle the foam with cinnamon, nutmeg or cocoa.

Variation
Prepare a cappuccino with the above recipe and put a dollop of
whipped cream on top of the foam. Sprinkle with cinnamon,
nutmeg or cocoa.

Café Latté
One part espresso and two or three parts foamed milk.

2 oz. espresso
6 oz. steamed milk
2 teaspoons milk foam

Cinnamon, nutmeg or cocoa

Combine espresso with milk. Add two tablespoons of milk
foam and sprinkle with cinnamon, nutmeg or cocoa.

Latté Macchiato
A small, but very tasty drink.

2 oz. espresso
6 oz. steamed milk
2 teaspoons milk foam

Place the milk and foam into a glass and gently pour in espresso. The difference with the above recipe is that the espresso will be between the foam and milk without mixing. The key to achieve this is to gently pour in the espresso. It will deposit on top of the milk.

Mochaccino
The perfect balance of coffee and chocolate.

4 oz. espresso
6 oz. milk
2 tablespoons chocolate syrup
Whipped cream
Cocoa or grated chocolate to taste
1 cherry

Combine milk with chocolate syrup and foam it with steam from the espresso maker. Now heat the mixture. When completely heated, pour the espresso into the demitasse and top with whipped cream, cocoa or grated chocolate and a cherry.

Belgian Espresso

4 oz. espresso
1 egg white
1 tablespoon sugar
1 tablespoon whipping cream
1/4 teaspoon vanilla
4 oz. steamed milk
Grated chocolate (optional)

Beat the egg white with the sugar until you get a meringue. Combine 1 tablespoon of meringue with 1 tablespoon whipped cream. Serve hot milk in a cup, add the meringue mixture over the milk. Finally, make a hole in the centre of the meringue and then pour the espresso through it. Garnish with grated chocolate, if desired.

Flat White

Originated in Australia, Flat White is a shot of espresso covered by a thin layer of micro foam. Micro foam is the fine foam that is found at the bottom of the container after frothing the milk with steam. The foam from the top is used for cappuccino and latté. The micro foam is more shinny and of a velvety consistency.

2 oz. espresso
6 oz milk

Heat milk and froth it. Pour the milk into a coffee cup. Pour espresso over the milk. Top with a thin layer of micro foam.

Mocha Cooler
You will feel great with this drink.

2 or 3 tablespoons chocolate syrup
1/2 cup milk
8 oz. cold espresso
1/2 teaspoon vanilla
Sweetened whipped cream

Dissolve the chocolate syrup in milk. Add the espresso and vanilla. Pour into 2 tall glasses with ice. Garnish with whipped cream.

Cappuccino Cooler
For a relaxing evening.

1/2 banana
2 oz. espresso
1 scoop of coffee ice cream
3/4 cup crushed ice
Whipped cream
Ground cinnamon

Beat the banana, espresso, ice cream and ice in blender. Serve in a tall glass. Garnish with whipped cream and cinnamon.

Cold Caramel Mochaccino

Very hot right now

1 tablespoon chocolate syrup
1 tablespoon caramel-flavoured syrup
2 oz. espresso
3/4 cup milk
1 cup crushed ice
Whipped cream

Mix milk, espresso and syrups in blender. Add crushed ice while blending. Serve in a tall glass. Garnish with whipped cream and a drizzle of caramel syrup over the cream.

Mocha Soda

Another cold delight.

2 oz. cold espresso
3 tablespoons chocolate syrup
2 tablespoons milk
1/2 teaspoon vanilla
2 scoops coffee ice cream
1/2 cup of cold mineral water
Whipped cream
Grated chocolate

Mix espresso, chocolate syrup, milk and vanilla in a tall glass. Add the ice cream. Fill the glass with mineral water. Mix gently. Garnish with whipped cream and grated chocolate.

Espresso with Soda
Delicious and refreshing.

2 oz. cold espresso
2 oz cold milk
Crushed ice
1 oz. mineral water
1 scoop vanilla or coffee ice cream

Serve espresso and milk in a glass with crushed ice. Add mineral water and ice cream.

Cooking with Coffee

Coffee is not only used to prepare beverages. Its earthy and slightly bitter flavour spice up many different dishes.

Grilled Steaks

Serves 6

6 beef steaks
1/4 cup vegetable oil
2/3 cup coffee
1 tsp mustard
3 cloves of garlic, pressed
1/2 teaspoon rosemary
1 teaspoon salt
1/2 teaspoon pepper

Mix all the ingredients and let the steaks marinate for 4 hours, turning them occasionally.
Cook over the barbecue fire until the steaks are done.

Chicken in Coffee Sauce

2 chicken breasts cut in half
a little flour
2 tablespoons of butter or margarine
1 cup of water
1 cup of coffee
3 tablespoons of flour

Season to taste and flour the chicken breasts. Fry them in a little oil until slightly golden. Remove from pan.
Add 2 tablespoons butter to the pan, let it melt, add 3 tablespoons flour, stir to blend with the butter and let it cook until golden brown. Remove from the heat and ad the water a little at a time stirring to combine with the mixture of flour and butter, add the coffee, mix well and return to the heat stirring constantly. When it starts to boil lower the heat and add the chicken. Cook for 10 more minutes and serve.

Coffee Pot Roast

3 lb. Chuck roast
4 garlic cloves pressed
1 large onion, chopped
2 tbsp olive oil
4 cups hot coffee
1 teaspoon salt
1/4 teaspoon pepper
1 tablespoon vinegar

Mix the pressed garlic with vinegar, salt and pepper to form a paste and rub the meat with it. Let it rest in the fridge covered for at least two hours.

Heat the oil in a large roaster. Brown the meat. Add the onion, let it caramelize. Add the coffee. Bake at 165° C (325° F) until the meat is fork tender. It could take 2 to 3 hours. Add potatoes and carrots around the meat in the last 45 minutes.

Chicken Casserole

2 chicken breasts halved
1/2 cup flour
Salt and pepper
1/2 cup of coffee
2 tablespoons oil
2 tablespoons butter

Mix flour with salt and pepper and coat the chicken pieces. Heat the oil and butter and fry the chicken until golden brown. Remove the chicken from the pan and add the remaining flour to the pan. Cook stirring for about 2 or 3 minutes. Remove from the heat. Add the coffee a little at a time stirring to combine. Cook stirring constantly and add water if it gets too thick. Add the chicken, and the vegetables and simmer covered until vegetables are tender. Add the cinnamon at the last minute.

Irresistible Desserts Made with Coffee

There is nothing more delicious than a homemade dessert accompanied by a steaming cup of coffee.

In this section, you will find different types of desserts. All the recipes are adaptations of popular desserts made with coffee. Coffee gives desserts a touch of magic by transforming them from great into something spectacular.

Any recipe that calls for chocolate can become mocha by substituting a little of the liquid with a little espresso or very strongly brewed coffee. In other recipes you can change the flavouring extract (almond or vanilla) for coffee, while eliminating a little of some other liquid.

Dare to experiment! You will enjoy the results.

Muffins

Muffins have their secrets. Mix dry ingredients and liquid ingredients separately and then combine the two mixtures. Do not over mix dry and liquid ingredients. The batter should be slightly lumpy.

Date and Coffee Muffins
Great for coffee breaks or mid-morning.

(Makes 12)

2/3 cup of hot coffee, prepared very strong
1 cup chopped dates
2/3 cup butter
1 cup brown sugar
2 eggs
1 1/2 cups flour
1/2 teaspoon baking soda
1 teaspoon baking powder
1/4 teaspoon salt

Preheat oven to 180° C (350° F)
Grease muffin pans or use paper muffin cups.
Soak dates in warm coffee for 20 minutes to soften.

Beat butter and brown sugar until it becomes creamy. Add the eggs one by one, beating well after every addition. Add coffee and dates. Mix well.

Sift the dry ingredients. Add to the liquid mixture gradually, stirring without beating, until everything is moistened.

Pour into prepared muffin pans and bake for 20 minutes.

Coffee and Walnut Muffins
Easy and delicious.

(Makes 12)

1/2 cup strong brewed coffee
1/2 cup milk
1 egg, beaten
1/2 cup melted butter
1 1/2 cups flour
2 1/2 teaspoons baking powder
1/3 cup sugar
1/4 teaspoon salt
1/2 cup chopped walnuts

Preheat oven to 180° C (350° F).
Grease muffin pans or use paper muffin cups.
Mix coffee with milk, egg and melted butter.
Sift dry ingredients.
Pour liquid mixture over dry mixture.
Add walnuts and mix until everything is well moistened.
Pour by spoonful into prepared pans. Do not fill more than 3/4 full.

Bake for 20 minutes.

Coffee and Coconut Muffins
Exotic combination.

(Makes 12)

1/2 cup butter at room temperature
1/2 cup sugar
1/2 cup brown sugar
2 eggs
1 3/4 cups flour
2 1/2 teaspoons baking powder
1/4 teaspoon salt
1/2 cup strong brewed coffee, cold
1/3 cup milk
2 teaspoons vanilla
1 1/2 cups chopped pecans
3/4 cup shredded coconut

Preheat oven to 180° C (350° F)

Grease muffin pans or use paper muffin cups.
Sift flour, baking powder and salt.
In another bowl, combine coffee, milk and vanilla.
Cream the butter with sugar and brown sugar.
Add the eggs one by one, beating well after each addition. Add coffee and milk mixture and combine well.
Add dry ingredients stirring without beating until everything is moistened.
Fill molds and bake for 30 minutes. Cool on a wire rack.
Serve warm with butter.

Tiramisu

A famous traditional Italian dessert included on the menus of the best restaurants in the world. This dessert is so ethereal that it is like travelling to heaven on a cloud.

(10 servings)

3 egg yolks
1 egg, separated
3 tablespoons icing sugar
1 1/3 cup Marsala or a good brandy
1/4 cup of freshly brewed espresso or very strong brewed coffee
250 g. Mascarpone cheese
1 teaspoon lemon juice
1/2 cup whipping cream
48 Lady Fingers
Cocoa, for garnish

Beat the 4 yolks with the icing sugar over a simmering double boiler until puffy.
Add 1/3 of wine or brandy, beating constantly until mixture begins to thicken.
Beat Mascarpone cheese with lemon juice and coffee, until you get a smooth paste.
Beat the egg white until peaks form, add it to the yolk mixture.
Whip cream until doubled in volume and thickened.
Dip half of the Lady Fingers in the remaining wine or brandy and arrange them in bottom of a 10 inch baking dish.
Cover with half the cheese mixture, then half the egg mixture and half the whipped cream.
Repeat layers of Lady Fingers, cheese mixture, egg and whipped cream.
Sprinkle cocoa over the whipped cream and refrigerate at least 4 hours.

Sacher Torte

The most famous Viennese chocolate cake–ideal pairing with a melange coffee.

1/2 cup unsalted butter
1/2 cup sugar
6 egg yolks
6 squares semi-sweet baking chocolate, melted and cooled
3/4 cup sifted flour
1/4 cup ground almonds
8 egg whites
1/2 cup sugar
1/2 cup peach jam
2 tablespoons cold water
6 squares semi-sweet baking chocolate, chopped
3/4 cup whipping cream
1/2 cup sugar
2 tablespoons corn syrup
2 tablespoons butter
1/2 cup peach syrup
1/2 cup sliced almonds
1 cup fresh whipped cream

Preheat oven to 180° C (350° F)

Cake

Beat butter and sugar until creamed. Add the yolks one by one, beating well after each addition.
Melt chocolate in a double boiler, cool and add to creamed butter. Mix well.
Combine flour with ground almonds. Beat egg whites until soft peaks form (for best results add 1/4 teaspoon cream of tartar to egg whites). Add 1/2 cup sugar gradually, beating until you get a stiff meringue.

Add 1/3 of the flour and almond mixture to the butter and egg yolk mixture. Mix gently. Add 1/3 of the meringue and mix gently. Continue blending in this way.

Butter two 9 inch pans and line them with a circle of waxed paper. Butter and sprinkle them with flour. Pour the mixture into the pans and bake for 30 to 35 minutes or until toothpick inserted in centre comes out clean.

Cool completely and invert. Remove waxed paper from loaves.

Peach Jam

Pass the jam through a sieve. Place in a saucepan. Add water and place over very low heat for 2 to 3 minutes. Spread half of warm jam over the first layer of cake. Put another layer on top and spread the other part of the jam over it.

Chocolate Frosting

Melt chocolate in a double boiler. Add cream, sugar and corn syrup and simmer over low heat for one minute without letting it boil, stirring occasionally. Remove from heat and add butter. Whisk the chocolate into the pot with a wooden spoon. Make sure chocolate is smooth and shiny and still is soft enough to spread over the cake.

Cover the cake with chocolate frosting using a spatula previously dipped in cold water.

Garnish the cake with canned peaches and sliced almonds. Refrigerate for 2 to 3 hours. Remove from refrigerator a half hour or an hour before serving.

Serve with sweetened whipped cream.

Brownies
They are very popular and easy to prepare.

Espresso Brownies
These brownies will make you famous and your friends will visit more often!

(Makes 16 squares)

1/2 cup butter
6 oz. bittersweet chocolate, grated or minced
1/4 cup espresso or very strong brewed coffee
2 eggs
3/4 cup sugar
2 teaspoons vanilla
3/4 cup flour
1/2 teaspoon baking powder
1/8 teaspoon baking soda
1 cup chopped walnuts

Frosting:

1 oz. bittersweet chocolate, grated or chopped
1 tablespoon butter
1 1/2 tablespoons espresso or very strong brewed coffee
3/4 cup sifted icing sugar
1 teaspoon finely ground coffee

Preheat oven to 160° C (320° F)
Grease a 8 inches square pan.
Melt butter and chocolate over low heat or in microwave, stirring occasionally.
Add espresso and let cool slightly.
Beat eggs with sugar until they are pale and thick.
Add vanilla and chocolate mixture, beat until smooth.
Add flour, baking powder and baking soda. Continue beating until smooth. Add the chopped walnuts.

Mix with a spatula.
Pour the mixture into the pan, smooth the surface and bake for 40 to 45 minutes or until a toothpick inserted in centre comes out clean.
Cool on a wire rack for 2 hours.

Frosting

Melt chocolate and butter. Add coffee and icing sugar gradually. When the mixture is spreadable stop adding icing sugar.
When cake is cool cover it with frosting. Refrigerate for at least 30 minutes before cutting it into 2 inches squares.

Coffee Ice Cream

Freshly roasted coffee gives this superb ice cream a delicate flavour.

(1-1/4 litres Approx.)

4 cups whipping cream
3/4 cup finely ground coffee
8 egg yolks
1 cup sugar

Heat the cream over low heat, add ground coffee, cover and remove from heat. Let stand for 20 minutes. Strain with a sieve and warm it again.
Beat egg yolks with sugar until they turn pale yellow. Place scoops of cream into the egg yolk mixture and fold them in gently. Continue adding cream to the egg yolk mixture until you have mixed in half of it. Pour yolk and cream mixture over the rest of the cream and cook over medium heat, stirring continuously until the cream thickens.
Pour into a bowl and place it in ice. When cold put it in the ice cream maker and proceed according to the manufacturer's instructions.

Coffee Jello

This is Kypogo's favourite dessert.

1/2 cup of cold coffee
3 envelopes unflavoured gelatin
3 1/2 cups of freshly brewed coffee
1/3 cup of sugar
Whipped cream

Let the gelatin soften in 1/2 cup of cold coffee for 3 minutes, then mix it into the hot coffee.
Stir until the gelatin is dissolved. Add the sugar and continue stirring until it is dissolved.
Place the gelatin mixture into a dish and chill.
When quite cold and almost jellied, beat up until it becomes a light foam.
Pour into a mold and place it in the fridge.
Serve with whipped cream.

Tip: A metal dish chills faster than a glass or plastic dish.

Coffee Legends and Curiosities

This book should not end without some legends and other interesting facts about coffee.

The Myth of Kaldi

Since coffee arrived in the western world, many legends have been told. A classic example is the one that tells of its discovery.

An Ethiopian shepherd named Kaldi was amazed at the behaviour of his goats after eating the leaves and fruits of certain shrubs. The goats jumped from one place to another and were more active than usual. Out of curiosity Kaldi tried those small fruits, like cherries, and felt more energetic and that night he had trouble sleeping.

The next day he told his wife about the strange behaviour of his goats and how he felt after eating the fruits. His wife advised him to take some of those fruits to the monastery and tell the monks about his experience. The monks listened with curiosity and one of them tasted the fruit, but he did not like the bitter taste and threw them into the fire that was near him.

When the coffee beans burned, they gave off a pleasant aroma. This was how the monks decided to roast the beans, make an infusion with them and drink the coffee during long periods of prayer to stay awake.

Satan's Brew

It is said that in the early seventeenth century some Christian fanatics pressured Pope Clement VIII to ban the black and luxuriant drink that by then had many adherents.

The Pope, who was an intelligent and wise man, decided to taste the drink before making his decision. After the first sip he exclaimed:

"It would be a sin to leave the infidels so delicious a drink. Let's defeat Satan by imparting the blessing to coffee to make it a Christian beverage."

This was how the Catholic Church baptized coffee and it ceased to be the drink of Satan.

The Most Expensive Coffee

The most expensive and rare coffee is known by the trade name of Kopi Luwak. It originates from the stool of a mammal called a civet, a close relative of the mongoose. This singular animal is native to the forests of Indonesia and loves the ripe fruits of coffee plants. However, the civet is unable to digest the beans, so they are expelled intact in its stools. Locals collect the beans as they know the high market value for them.

Vienna and its Passion for Coffee

According to legend, the addiction of the Viennese people to coffee dates back to the second half of the seventeenth century. Vienna had been invaded by the Turks and when they were expelled from the city they abandoned, among other things, sacks of green coffee beans. The beans were roasted and the Viennese prepared coffee with them. Thereafter, the glamourous coffee houses came, and soon they became the centre of Vienna's social life.

Statue of Franz George Kolschitzky, Patron Sait of Vienna Coffee Lovers. Erected by the Coffee Makers Guild of Vienna.

From "All About Coffee" by William H. Ukers, 1922.

The King Who Banned Coffee

A Swedish legend tells that in the late eighteenth century, King Gustav III decided to ban coffee in his kingdom because he considered it a poison. There were many protests and in order to calm the people he ordered a clinical trial to demonstrate that coffee was harmful to health and that people would die if they continued drinking it.

For the clinical trial two doctors and two death row inmates were appointed. The test would consist in giving one of the prisoners a good dose of coffee and the other, tea.

The results ... the doctors died first, the king was murdered and the prisoners had a long life. The one who drank tea died at the age of 83. No age was given for the coffee drinker, but he is said to have lived several years longer than his fellow inmate.

How Coffee Arrived in Brazil

According to a picturesque and romantic legend in 1727, the emperor of Brazil sent Francisco de Mello Palheta to French Guinea in search of coffee seeds to cultivate throughout his empire. The French did not want to share this valuable asset with other colonies in America, so when de Mello Palheta told the governor of French Guinea his intention to begin the cultivation of coffee in Brazil, the governor flatly refused to provide seeds. De Mello Palheta had no intention of returning to Brazil empty handed. After some pondering, he decided on a completely different approach to getting what he wanted: He decided to seduce the governor's wife. His strategy worked, and at the farewell party the governor had organized, he received a bouquet of flowers in which the governor's wife had hidden some coffee beans. These seeds came to Brazil and were planted and flourished like nowhere else due to favourable climate and soil conditions, making Brazil a major force in the production of coffee.

Coffee in Music and Films

Coffee is part of everyday life, and this is reflected in songs and movies. In the U.S., there is a substantial discography with references to coffee. In our research we found more than 100 recordings in which coffee is mentioned. One of the famous and remembered songs was recorded by Nat *"King"* Cole in the twenties *"You are the Cream in my Coffee"*. Frank Sinatra recorded in 1946 the *"Coffee Song"*. Ella Fitzgerald performed *"Black Coffee"* in 1948.

In the 60s, there were a number of popular songs: *"Coffee Blues"* by Mississippi John Hurt and *"Cigarettes and Coffee"* by Otis Redding, to name just a couple. Those tunes and many others have been recorded in a variety of formats: heavy 78 rpm discs, LP's 33 1/2 rpm, cassettes and CDs.

On YouTube there is an inspirational video that compares life with coffee. It is called *"Life is Like a Cup of Coffee"* www.youtube.com/watch?v=U3NgzQ9Pcsg

There are countless references to coffee in films. *"Casablanca"*, one of the most famous films ever made and winner of three Oscars in 1942, has a memorable line about coffee:

"Thanks for the coffee Signor Ferrari. I will miss your coffee when I leave Casablanca". Ingrid Bergman (1915-1982) as Ilsa Lund.

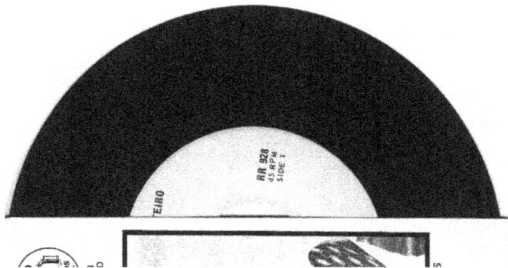

Coffee Art

In 2010 the Lake Country ArtWalk Festival's theme was coffee. There were lots of artists exhibiting their works, many of them were coffee related. The Festival had coffee painted, sculpted, sung, filmed and specially written in interesting books.

The Lake Country ArtWalk is the largest art show in the Okanagan.

Coffee Fountain at the ArtWalk in Lake Country, BC, Canada.

Suspended Coffee

Suspended Coffee is not a new drink sold at coffee shops. It is a movement that is spreading around the world.

This is a great concept, an act of kindness that can brighten the day of many people. You go to a participating coffee shop and purchase your coffee and you can also purchase a Suspended Coffee. The Suspended Coffee is not for you, it is a cup of coffee that will be given to a person who cannot afford it. The person doesn't have to prove anything, he or she just has to ask for it: "can I have a cup of Suspended Coffee please?" And he or she will get a cup of coffee paid by an anonymous person.

The Suspended Coffee movement is not new. It started in Italy some years ago and it has spread from there to many countries in Europe and North America and recently to Australia and the Philippines.

Coffee on the Web

Internet Cafes - Coffee on the Web

The first *cyber cafe* opened in England in 1994 and later more opened in other cities in Europe, USA, Canada, Australia, Latin America and some Asian countries. In some Internet cafes people can drink a reasonable cup of coffee. All Internet cafes have computers with Internet access for guests to make use of this technology. It is worth mentioning that in most countries the Internet cafes offer Internet service but do not offer coffee. In fact, in third world countries they are the only facilities with Internet access, but the name *Internet Cafe* has stuck.
There is an abundance of information about Internet cafes. We suggest you visit **www.cybercafe.com**. This site contains a database of 4208 internet cafes in 141 countries.

Frequently asked questions about coffee and caffeine are at **www.coffeefaq.com**.

A trip to the world of coffee can be found at **www.cafedecolombia.com**. This site contains information about coffee, its history, coffee prices, preparation, recipes, and Juan Valdez, the famous Colombian coffee logo. The page is maintained by the National Federation of Coffee Growers of Colombia.

The Brazilian Association of Coffee Industry (ABIC) **www.abic.com.br** promotes programs to improve the quality of coffee in Brazil, its services and also publishes statistics and news about coffee.

International coffee organizations also have an Internet presence. On the website of the International Coffee Organization (ICO) **www.ico.org** you can find the history of coffee, the objectives of this organization, the members, statistics and data on caffeine, botany, and information about courses and seminars it offers.

Specialty Coffee Association of America (SCAA) **www.scaa.org** offers courses, conferences, discussion forums, barista competitions, and an extensive library on coffee.

Tea and Coffee Trade Journal (TCTJ) **www.teaandcoffee.net** contains interesting information about world coffee, programs to improve coffee quality, coffee and health, and statistics on coffee.

Another important source is in Zurich, Switzerland: **Library-Museum Jacobs-Suchard**. It is the most important museum of the history of coffee. Jacobs-Suchard museum includes items from the seventeenth century to the present. **www.jacobsfoundation.org**

All websites mentioned in this chapter were visited March 2013.

Final Note

If you have questions, comments or if you wish to order copies
of this book, please email kypogo@gmail.com

www.ingramcontent.com/pod-product-compliance
Lightning Source LLC
Chambersburg PA
CBHW022307060426
42446CB00007BA/741